I0085013

"GRACE"

It Is NOT What You Think.

By Dr.AL Garza

Published by Sefer Press

Sefer Press
Publishing House

Copyright 2018
All Rights Reserved

Publication rights Sefer Press Publishing House
Questions & Comments; SeferPress@israelmail.com

Cover by Sefer Press 2018

Book Format by Sefer Press 2018

ISBN: 978-0692113677

For questions or comments, please write to

SeferPress@israelmail.com

Bible Abbreviations

Some Bible translations is that of the author who
translated from the Hebrew and Greek language.

Printed in the United States of America 2018

TABLE OF CONTENTS

Introduction…………………………...pg.4

Noah is Grace…………………………pg.6

Grace in Hebrew……………………pg.9

The Rest of the Old Testament…......pg.12

The New Testament...........................pg.17

Conclusion..pg.32

INTRODUCTION

Grace, *"A masculine noun meaning favor, grace, acceptance. Meaning an unmerited favor or regard in God's sight."* This is the most common understanding of the word "grace" in our pulpits today. Every modern preacher I have seen on TV and heard on the radio has given that meaning while preaching. Even in most concordances and lexicons, that meaning is conveyed. But where does that word come from in the Bible? What is the origin of the word "grace" and what was the true meaning and understanding of the word? Before the New Testament was written how did the Jews

understand "grace" from the Hebrew Bible?
Most Christian believers will be shocked to
learn that "grace" did not have the meaning of
"unmerited favor" as understood today.

NOAH IS GRACE

When God was about to destroy the earth by a flood, he spoke to Noah and told him to make an ark and put his family inside of it for safety. God warned Noah and protected him and his family from the flood. But why?

Gen.6:8 ונח מצא **חֵן** בעיני יהוה (Bold Hebrew letters for the name *Noah* and *favor*)
"But Noah found favor (grace) in the eyes of YHVH."

The word "favor" in Genesis 6:8 is the word *grace* that is used to teach unmerited favor. Genesis 6:8 is the first time we see the

ט

word *grace* used in the Hebrew Bible. But there is something in the Hebrew that you cannot see in the English translations. First, let me point out that Noah *found* or as the literal Hebrew puts it, *attained/acquired* favor or grace. The Hebrew word מצא (matsa) is best translated as attained or acquired. Noah acquired favor/grace from God. Does that sound like unmerited favor? How did Noah acquire favor or grace?

אלה תולדת נח נח איש צדיק תמים Gen.6:9

היה בדרתיו את־האלהים התהלך־נח

"These are the generations of Noah. Noah was a righteous man, blameless in his generation. Noah walked with God." (ESV)

Noah attained or acquired grace from God because he had a relationship with God. Noah was a truthful man who walked with God. Therefore God instructed him to build an ark for his protection. We also read this in Genesis 7:1,

*"Then YHVH said to Noah, "Go into the ark, you and all your household, for **I have seen that you are righteous before me in this generation**."*

Noah acted righteously before YHVH and YHVH saw and gave him protection or grace. But what about the word *grace*?

GRACE IN HEBREW

The Hebrew word for grace is חֵן (CheN) with

two Hebrew letters, the C*het* and the N*un*. In

ancient Hebrew, the letters represented a word

and a picture. The first letter in the Hebrew

word for *grace* represents a fence that

surrounds and protects. Therefore, the Hebrew

picture for *chet* looks like a fence. And the

second Hebrew letter, the *nun*, means life or to

propagate, Psalm 72:17, and the Hebrew word

picture resembles a symbol for life. Both

Hebrew letters can be found in the Hebrew

Bible as a word by themselves. Now, if we take

that same Hebrew word for *grace*, *CheN*, and

write it backward, it will spell the Hebrew name for Noah. The *Nun* and the *Chet* combined make the name Noah in English. So, Noah in the eyes of YHVH, like a backward reflection, makes the word grace or favor in Hebrew. Noah (Nun, Chet) attained or acquired grace (Chet, Nun) in the eyes of YHVH. This makes sense in the Hebrew word picture because Noah attained God's protection of his life by building the ark. The ark is a picture of grace, God's protection. This is the very foundation of the word *grace* or *favor* without the meaning of unmerited since Noah attained protection from God by having a personal relationship with him before the flood. The majority of Christians who believe "unmerited favor" teaching try very hard to explain this away because it does

not fit their theology of grace. Especially those

in the Reform movement.

THE REST OF THE OLD TESTAMENT

If we continue to follow the Hebrew word
for *grace* in the Old Testament, we will see a
pattern develop. In the entire first five books of
Moses, the Torah, the word *grace* or *favor* is
always preceded by the word "found" which in
Hebrew means *attained* or *acquired*. This is
also true in the Writings and the Prophets until
we get to Psalms and Proverbs. The English
Bible translators begin to translate the Hebrew
word for grace as graceful, adornment and
charm. About 95%+ of the entire Hebrew
Bible reads, "...found favor..." or more
literally, "...attained/acquired

favor/protection…" The Jewish and Hebrew understanding was that an individual could attain God's protection and mercy. The phrase was also understood and used toward kings and men in the Hebrew Old Testament. It was never defined or interpreted as unmerited favor. If one reads merely and follows the Hebrew word throughout the Old Testament, you cannot help but see the pattern. Here are some examples.

Gen.18:3 *"and said, (Abraham) "O Lord, if I have **found favor** in **your sight**, do not pass by your servant."*

Gen.19:19 (Lot speaking) *"Behold, your servant has **found favor** in **your sight**, and you have shown me great kindness in saving my life. But I cannot escape to the hills, lest the disaster overtake me, and I die."*

Exo.33:12 *"Moses said to the LORD, "See, you say to me, 'Bring up these people,' but you have not let me know whom you will send with me. Yet you have said, 'I know you by name, and you have also **found favor** in **my sight**.'"*

Jdg.6:17 *"So Gideon said to Him, "If now I have **found favor** in **Your sight**, then show me a sign that it is You who speak with me."*

These are just a few passages that show part of the 95%+ of texts that prove my findings. The Old Testament Hebrew Bible supports that *favor* or *grace* is not grounded in the teaching of unmerited favor. Any person can search out for themselves the passages that are part of the 95%+ and see the pattern of the phrase "*…found favor in your sight…*" So, what about the New Testament? Does it support the unmerited favor teaching?

NOTE: The word "grace" in Hebrew is never connected with receiving eternal life. In other words, "grace" does not equal eternal life. It is used to convey God's protection and blessing to his people who follow his commandments or Torah. If they do not keep his word, then grace (God's blessing and protection) is removed, and they will be put under God's curse. Also, the Hebrew word "CheN" for *grace* is translated in the Greek LXX as "charin" which is the same as the New Testament Greek word "charis" or "chariti."

THE NEW TESTAMENT

As we come to the New Testament, we must remember that all we have, for the most part, are Greek copies and fragments. The Greek is not the same as Hebrew. Greek is an abstract language that comes from Semitic languages. Hebrew is concrete and is based on pictures and words for each letter while Greek does not. With that note, let us look at one of the foundation verse that is used to teach unmerited favor/grace in the New Testament. It comes from Ephesians 2:8-9.

Eph.2:8-9 *"For by grace you have been saved through faith. And this is not your own doing;*

it is the gift of God, not a result of works, so

that no one may boast."

This verse is part of the foundation for "unmerited favor" teaching. But how do we get the word *grace* translated into these verses? It is a body of scholars who come together to decide how to translate the Hebrew and the Greek into English that will be easier to read for the reader. In Ephesians 2:8 we see the word *grace* in the passage. But does that word mean *unmerited favor* in Greek? How is it translated in the rest of the New Testament? The Greek word for *grace* in Ephesians 2:8 is χάρις (charis). The shock to most Christian believers will be that *charis* is not always translated *grace* with the understanding of unmerited favor. In the New American Standard Bible, the Greek word *charis* is translated *gracious work* in 2Corinthias,

2Co.8:6-7 *"So we urged Titus that as he had previously made a beginning, so he would also complete in you this **gracious work** as well. But just as you abound in everything, in faith and utterance and knowledge and in all earnestness and in the love, we inspired in you, see that you abound in this **gracious work** also."* (NASB)

One translation, the ESV, has "act of grace" while others translate with

either *grace* or *work*. In fact, within the New Testament, we find the Greek word being translated in numerous ways. We see the translation of *credit, benefit, blessing, thanks, gratitude, concession*, etc. The Greek word is never used to mean just grace. Why? If this word is supposed to mean "unmerited favor" in connection with eternal life and salvation, then why does it change in meaning when used in other verses? This answer is simple. Men have decided to translate the Greek word into *grace* into the verses they believe it has the meaning of the unmerited favor teaching.

Ephesians 2:8 can be translated as follows,

Eph. 2:8-9 *"For **by His gracious work** you have been saved through faith. And this is not your own doing; it is the gift of God, not a result of works (your works), so that no one may boast."*

This translation can efficiently work because Jesus did all the work for us by fulfilling the Torah and dying on the cross for the atonement of sins. We are blessed with eternal life through and by his works and not by ours. Remember, the Old Testament is the foundation for the New Testament and both need to be consistent and in harmony. If we understand that *grace* is

a blessing and work from God to us for eternal

life, then it fits the consistency of the Old

Testament usage as well. Even in Romans, the

word grace can be retranslated and still fit

perfectly with how we receive eternal life.

Rom.3:23 *"…for all have sinned and fall short*

of the glory of God, and are justified by

his **grace** *as a gift, through the redemption that*

is in Christ Jesus,"

Rom.3:23 *"…for all have sinned and fall short*

of the glory of God, and are justified by

his **gracious work/blessing** *as a gift, through*

the redemption that is in Christ Jesus,"

Both passages are true if we understand grace to mean, not unmerited favor, but God's work and blessing in our lives. We are justified by the work of Jesus as a gift to us. But for us to receive this blessing from God by his work through Jesus, we need to have faith and believe in the one who completed the work. Therefore Jesus can be full of grace or blessings and how we can fall from grace or his blessings. Below are more examples how the Greek word *charis* is translated in most Bibles and others retranslated by me.

Luk.6:32 *"But if you love those who love you, what **credit** is that to you? For even sinners love those, who love them."* (English Majority Text Version) See also verse 33-34, "*credit.*"

Luk.17:9 *"Does he **thank** the servant because he did what was commanded?"* (ESV)

Act.18:27 *"And when he wished to cross to Achaia, the brothers encouraged him and wrote to the disciples to welcome him. When he arrived, he greatly helped those who through **grace [His gracious work]** had believed,"* (My translation added)

Rom.1:5 *"Through Christ, God gave me the **special work** of an apostle—to lead people of all nations to believe and obey him. I do all this to honor Christ."* (Easy To Read Version)

Rom.3:24 *"being justified as a gift by His **grace [gracious work]** through the redemption which is in Christ Jesus;"* (NASB-brackets added)

Gal.2:21 *"I do not nullify the **grace [The work/blessing]** of God, for if righteousness were through the law, then Christ died for no purpose."* (ESV-brackets added)

I can continue to post verse after verse showing that if we consider the Greek word *charis* to be understood as gracious work, blessing with God's protection that all still fit the context and the meaning from the Old Testament. In many of the New Testament salutations we see "…grace and peace…" or "The grace of our Lord Jesus…" which is better understood from the Hebrew old Testament greetings of "Blessings…" We should be translating those New Testament verses "…blessings and peace…" and "The blessings of our Lord Jesus…" This fits best when we consider the Jewish understanding of the Hebrew Bible. The word "grace" in the New Testament has been overused dramatically that it has lost its true meaning which is grounded in the Genesis 6:8 and the rest of the Old Testament. The challenge will be to abandon the modern tradition of "unmerited favor" or something for nothing teaching and realize that God grants us eternal life by our faith and trust in him through Jesus the Messiah. In doing so, we receive his blessings and protection in the form of grace and mercy. The teaching of eternal life comes from many New Testament verses with the condition of believing in Jesus as the son of man and as Messiah. In fact, the Gospel of John was written for this very purpose.

Joh.20:31 "*but these have been written so that you may believe that Jesus is the Christ,* the Son of God; and that **believing** you may

have **life in His name**." (NASB)

Joh.3:15 "...that whoever **believes** in him

(the son of man) may have **eternal life**."

(ESV)

Joh.6:40 "For this is the will of my Father,

that everyone who looks on the Son

and **believes** in him should have **eternal life**,

and I will raise him up on the last day." (ESV)

Joh.6:47 "Truly, truly, I say to you,

whoever **believes** has **eternal life**." (ESV)

In other parts of the New Testament, we see another connection to eternal life in regard to belief and seeking. This does not suggest that we receive eternal life by works. But there is an action on our part of coming to God in trust and faith regarding Jesus. To a Jew, trust and belief in Jesus as Messiah is NOT considered work as some may suppose.

Rom.2:7 *"…to those who by patience in well-doing seek for glory and honor and immortality, he will give **eternal life**;"* (ESV)

In other verses in the New Testament, we see the connection between eternal life and grace being used. Here are a couple of examples found in Romans and one in Titus.

Rom.5:21 "*...so that, as sin reigned in death, grace [His work/blessing] also might reign through righteousness leading to eternal life through Jesus Christ our Lord.*" (ESV)

Rom.6:23 "*For the wages of sin is death, but the gift [The work/blessing] of God is eternal life in Christ Jesus our Lord.*" (English Majority Test Version)

Tit.3:7 *"so that being justified by His **grace**
[His gracious work] we would be made heirs
according to the hope of **eternal life**."* (ESV)

Paul continues his teaching to Timothy
regarding eternal life by saying,

*"Yet for this reason, I found mercy, so that in
me as the foremost, Jesus Christ might
demonstrate His perfect patience as an
example for those who would **believe in Him
for eternal life**."* (1Timothy 1:16, NASB)

CONCLUSION

In conclusion, I want to make something very clear. I am not saying we as believers in Jesus the Messiah are saved or justified by the works that we do. Eternal life is in Jesus the Son of God, and by believing and trusting in him and the work, he has done for us. In doing so, we receive the blessing and protection of God in the form of grace and mercy which is the true meaning of *grace* in the New Testament and the Old Testament.

1Jn.5:11 *"And this is the testimony, that God gave us eternal life, and this life is in his Son."* (ESV) Amen and amen!

RESOURCES

RESOURCES

1. Timothy Ware. *The Orthodox Church, Revised Edition* Penguin Books, 1992. pp.239ff.

2. Matthew J. Slick. "The Five Points of Calvinism." September 7, 2009

3. Randy Maddox, *Responsible Grace* (Kingswood, 1994)

4. Paul F. M. Zahl, *Grace in Practice: A Theology of Everyday Life* (Eerdmans, 2007)

5. *Hebrew Word Pictures*, Hebrew World Inc. - Hebrew Heart Media; 5th - Brand new 2016-17 edition (2016)

6. *Strong's Concordance*, Thomas Nelson; Expanded edition (April 11, 2010)

7. *The Brown-Driver-Briggs Hebrew and English Lexicon*: With an Appendix Containing the Biblical Aramaic: Coded with the Numbering System from Strong's Exhaustive Concordance of the Bible Hardcover – June 1, 1996.

www.ingramcontent.com/pod-product-compliance
Lightning Source LLC
Chambersburg PA
CBHW071449040426
42445CB00012BA/1496